WINDOWS OF THOUGHT

AN ESSANDESS SPECIAL EDITION

NEW YORK

WINDOWS
OF
THOUGHT

Stillman J. Elwell

WINDOWS OF THOUGHT

SBN: 671-10540-X

Published by ESSANDESS SPECIAL EDITIONS,
a division of Simon & Schuster, Inc.,
630 Fifth Avenue, New York, N.Y. 10020,
and on the same day in Canada
by Simon & Schuster of Canada, Ltd.,
Richmond Hill, Ontario.

Printed in the U.S.A.
Designed by The Etheredges

To My Wife

CONTENTS

WAYS OF LIFE

Let others talk of roaring mills and mines
And of the clamor in the busy street,
Who haven't seen the meadows in the spring
And felt the fresh plowed earth beneath their feet.
Whose ears have not been tuned to those faint sounds
That come when earth in snow is buried deep,
Nor to the quiet patter on the roof
As gentle rain has lulled them off to sleep.

But let me tell of earth and cloud and sky
And of the first faint glory on the hill,
When autumn knocks, unheard, at summer's gate
And Time itself, it seems, is standing still,
And Time's own miracle that turns a field
With magic touch, from green to shining gold,
The while the woodland and the hedges bloom
Then don their scarlet when the year is old.

Yes, let them speak of other ways of life
Who haven't seen the glory of the sun
In splendor sinking in the western hills
When summer's golden day, at last, is done!
Who haven't stood enraptured in the night
And watched a thousand outer worlds roll by,
Who haven't felt the grandeur of the stars
And seen the Hand of God across the sky!

SLEIGH TRACKS

I am lost in the whirlwind of gadgets and gears
That has changed this old world, with the passing of years,
From the world of contentment and peace that I knew,
To a place of confusion—fantastic but true!

The old stove that so cozily toasted our knees,
While the rest of our bodies continued to freeze,
Is replaced in these days, in the homes of the land,
By a hole in the wall, that I can't understand!

And the horses that plodded so patiently on
Down the long country roads of my boyhood, are gone!
And it's far back indeed from our up-to-date ways
To the hard-beaten snow in the tracks of the sleighs!

For today, when we ride, we are up in the skies,
At three hundred per hour, in a gadget that flies;
And the hopes and the fears that we knew in the past
Have been blended in dread of the hydrogen blast!

So then pity a fellow who lived long ago,
And remembers the tracks in the hard-beaten snow,
And who's hopelessly lost in the gadgets and gears
That are left in the wake of the fast flying years.

Pity me, did I say? No, for happy am I
With a sleigh in the snow, or a jet in the sky,
With a horse on the ground or some gadget above,
If around me are gathered The Friends That I Love!

GREAT THINGS AND SMALL

If you're going to live at the edge of the pond
Where a winding path leads along the shore,
Don't boast of your trip on the ocean wide
To the friends and neighbors who live next door;
For the self-same sun sets on pond and sea,
And the self-same stars, on a moonless night,
Guide the traveler on in the winding path,
And the pilot, far on an ocean flight!

And the self-same God, in His Mighty Plan,
Made a thousand ponds for each storm-swept sea,
And it must have pleased Him that little things
Should be known of men and remembered be;
For these little things, as they're multiplied,
Make a mightier world than we'll ever know,
And the pond and the ocean are parts thereof,
And it must have pleased Him that this is so!

OLD MOTHER EARTH

One thing I know—When strife has ceased
And guns are stacked and still
And all the Gods of War and Hate
And Greed have had their fill—
This good old earth will send forth buds
Where shells are bursting now;
The stark and devastated lands
Shall feel again the plow.

The sun will set on blood red plains—
Its rays of morning greet
The hills that thundered to the tread
Of countless marching feet,
With heralds of a better dawn;
And men at least shall find,
Despite the havoc of their hate,
Old Mother Earth is kind!

OF THE HILLS

I like the loamy, fertile soil
That's found in level fields,
For after all 'tis level land
The greatest harvest yields.

And yet I cannot be content,
Tho' level be the way,
Unless my eyes behold the hills
At the closing of the day.

I like the city's bustling ways,
The noisy traffic song,
And in the busy thoroughfares
To mingle with the throng.

But in the hurry of the town,
Amid its pomp and frills;
God grant that I may not forget
That I am of the hills!

The hills that spread their broad expanse
Before my tired eyes,
The hills that soothe my troubled soul
And bear me to the skies!

I LOVE A YEAR

I love a year because it's born
When pale stars are aglow
And all the earth is fast asleep
In January's snow.

I love a year when bursting buds
Bedeck the hills of May
And field and forest turn to green
As rippling waters play.

And when the lazy summer sun
Sinks slowly out of sight,
My year is crowned, as dying day
Fades into purple night.

But death must take my lovely year;
And under autumn skies
It dons its gold and scarlet robe,
Majestic as it dies!

And after death—Ah, then my year
Has reached its goal sublime,
For then it stands at Heaven's Gate
And sings—at Christmas Time!

IT'S MAY

It's May! It's May! And the fields are gay
With the growing wheat and clover,
The laughing brook has a cheery look
For the winter's reign is over!

It's spring! It's spring! And the bluebirds sing,
In the azure heavens soaring,
The joyous notes from their tiny throats
In a wave of song out-pouring!

It's true! It's true! There's a life anew
And a fresh green world it's bringing,
Away with gloom when the orchards bloom
And the oriole is singing!

'Tis well! 'Tis well! That the song birds tell
Of a rapture overflowing,
The humblest clod sings the praise of God
When the breath of May is blowing!

SEPTEMBER'S MIRACLE

Yesterday the skies were hazy
And the fields were dusty gray
With the lazy drowse and languor
Of a hot late-summer day.

But a crimson brush has painted
With an artistry sublime,
And another day is ushered
On the fleeting wings of time.

Now the haze has turned to purple
And the dust to sparkling dew,
And the age-old hills are mantled
With a glory ever new.

And my spirit is enraptured
With a strange unanswered call;
Yesterday was waning summer,
But today is early fall!

AUTUMN'S GLORY

I have lived to see the glory
Of another autumn day,
And to view its crimson splendor on the hill,
To behold its sunset linger
On the slope across the way,
And to feel its spell when all the earth is still.

I have lived to know the autumn
Is a harbinger of spring,
That its ???????? ?????? ?? ???? ?? ??? ? ????,
That its thousand tongues, enraptured,
Of a resurrection sing,
And for this, Dear God, I thank you from my heart!

OCTOBER SUNSET

There's a sort o' solemn grandeur
On a bright October day,
When the lazy sun is shinin'
On the hills across the way,
When the sumac's turnin' crimson
An' the maple's all aflame
An' you realize the summer's
Playin' out a losin' game.

There's a wonder an' a glory
As the day draws to a close,
An' you know you're watchin' nature
In her mightiest o' shows,
When the crimson's turnin' purple
As the sun sinks out o' sight
An' a hush falls on the woodlands
As the day slips into night!

Watch an' listen then in rapture;
Hold that moment to the last,
For it's loaded down with grandeur
An' it's goin' all too fast;
But there's somethin' while it lingers
That approaches the sublime,
For it seems that God is nearer
Than at any other time!

EARTH'S GOODNESS

Tho' we may travel far e'er seeking rest,
Long seeking pleasure, finding naught but pain,
Earth turns no beaten wanderer from her breast,
But heals them with her sunshine and her rain.

Ah, gently closes o'er us when the hour
Of life's brief toil and struggle shall have passed,
As fades the tender petal of the flower
Before the icy chill of winter's blast.

Aye, sends forth buds above us while we sleep,
That through the clouds of turmoil and of care,
That shroud our earthly vision, they who weep
May see the symbol of a life more fair!

THE SNOWFLAKE

Just a tiny little snowflake,
Oddly fashioned it is true,
Shining brightly on the window,
White as lilies, pure as dew.

Ah! What mystery surrounds it,
In its drifts the children play,
Yet is locked the wealth of kingdoms
In its icy prisons gray.

Falling gently as a blanket,
Soft and sweet as babies' breath,
Or in swirling, raging madness,
Driving men to bitter death.

Trackless forests know its grandeur,
Barren wastes its fetters feel,
Mighty regions are imprisoned,
As it were with bonds of steel.

All the wisdom of the ages,
All the truths the sages know,
Come to naught before the power
Of the tiny flake of snow!

THE FOLKS I KNOW

The world, I hear, is going wrong,
Has struck a steep decline,
And on its sons, the star of hope,
Alas, has ceased to shine.

No honest men are found these days,
No noble women now;
The cynic's sneer replaced all smiles,
A frown on every brow.

No one reflects on things worthwhile,
All thought is base and mean,
All acts belong to realms of night,
Ungodly and unclean.

And so I go my weary way
In sorrow and alarm;
This wicked world, these evil folk,
Must surely come to harm.

And yet, no matter where I go,
A kindly face I see;
Someone is glad to be of help,
Someone is good to me.

Someone has lost all thought of self
In striving for the best,
Has faltered not though sorely tried,
Has stood the acid test.

Perhaps it's true the world's gone wrong
And folks are out of line,
And yet, how strange, the ones I know
Are all so good and fine!

GOOD FRIENDS

I held high hopes long years ago
Of winning wealth and fame;
All tasks were simple, so it seemed,
And life was just a game.

The error I so surely made
I found in course of time,
For life is stern and steep the path
Our weary feet must climb!

I read fine books and then forgot
The lessons therein found;
I saw great sights but left them all
When I was homeward bound.

And so 'twould seem that I have failed
In all I strove to do;
I gathered neither fame nor wealth
Nor knowledge, it is true.

My life has been a waste of time,
Perhaps I hear you say;
Ah no! For I have found and kept
Good friends along the way!

MIRACLES

No miracles? The sun goes down
Beyond the western hill,
The shadows fall, the breezes die,
The earth is hushed and still.

The mountains rear their lofty peaks
In triumph to the sky,
The great gray geese, when autumn comes
Know where and when to fly!

A man is born, grows old and dies
In quiet ordered way,
A guiding hand in his, the while
He lives his little day.

The fields are green, then gold, and white
All in their own good time,
The countless galaxies of stars
Perform their role sublime!

No miracles? Ah! Those good friends
Whose eyes have failed to see,
Are blind indeed, for all these things
Are miracles to me!

RICHES

I am sad for him who is rich in gold,
Who has counted cash till he's bent and old,
Who's exchanged a beautiful world of dreams
For a world of money and sordid schemes.

For he isn't rich where the drone of bees
And the songs of birds are in all the trees,
Where the cedars grow and the partridge feed;
He's a stranger there, and is poor indeed!

There's a rosebud nodding across the way,
And a meadow yonder with lambs at play,
And the sun, in splendor, is sinking low
In the purple hills—But he doesn't know!

He is poor indeed when the wild geese fly,
With their honking chains, in a leaden sky;
And he has no friends in the lakes and ponds—
He is rich, but only in Stocks and Bonds!

TIMELESS FRIENDS

They tell me that the dog is man's best friend,
And truly in the depths of those brown eyes
I see such adoration, I reflect
That here indeed is love mankind should prize.

And yet I know, in just a little while,
My dog must go the way all flesh must go,
And I shall mourn a friend beyond recall,
While yet I live, and hope, and dream and grow.

But I have other far less transient friends,
Old friends grown dearer with the passing years,
Good friends alike when joyous is my path,
And when my eyes are filled with bitter tears.

Majestic friends, unchanging since the time
When long ago, I drew my first faint breath;
Unchanging still when in the coming years
I take my journey in the realm of death!

What friends are these? They greet each coming morn,
And when the sun in splendor paints the west,
The glory of its fading light proclaims
Of all man's friends—The Hills and Trees are Best!

SHALL COME AGAIN

I couldn't see the apple blossoms falling,
Their tender petals floating on the breeze;
I couldn't bear to have the leaves of autumn
Fade, fall, and leave again the naked trees.

My eyes could ne'er behold the gold and purple,
The glory of the slowly setting sun,
The solemn hush that comes to earth at twilight,
When evening breeze proclaims—"The day is done."

My heart would break beneath the crushing sorrow
Of parting grief—'Twould never bear the pain,
Were not the thought, that in a glad tomorrow
Leaves, blossoms, life and love shall come again!

NATURE'S GRANDEUR

I would like to write a poem
To those friends who love a hill,
And who love to walk at evening
In the twilight dim and still;
Those who love the silent splendor
Of the summer sunset's glow,
And who walk with measured footsteps
In a world that's hushed with snow.

For to them belong the blossoms
That adorn the hills of May,
And the blaze of crimson glory
That we call an autumn day!
Theirs to love the ways of nature
And to call her creatures friends,
Theirs to view the changing seasons
With an awe that never ends!

So I dedicate my poem
To those friends who lift their eyes
To the glory of the sunset
And the beauty of the skies,
Who forget Life's sordid troubles,
Disappointments, pain and scars,
As they gaze in rapt amazement
At the grandeur of the stars!

SUNRISE

A glow lights up the eastern sky
As purple shadows fade,
And, sparkling in its coat of dew,
A fresh new world is made!

There's something in the rising sun
That casts a magic spell
Across the doorway of the heart—
At least that's what they tell!

And some day when I m strong and fit,
With nothing much to do,
I'm going to turn my bed around
So I Can See One Too!

SUNSET

I love to stand on a high old hill
As the sun is going down,
And watch the gold as it slowly fades
On the steeples of the town.

I love to gaze on the checkered fields
Spreading out below me there,
And feel the hush of the dying day
On the soft and balmy air.

But better still do I love to watch
As the purple edges high
Across the slopes of the neighbor hills,
Till it meets the evening sky.

What noble thoughts, what ecstatic dreams,
And what lofty visions rise
Within the soul as the sun goes down,
And at last the long day dies!

NEVER LOST

You may lose a song or story
And forget its lesson true,
Lose the fickle fame and glory
That the years are bringing you;
Money you have earned and hoarded
You may never live to spend,
Health may fade Time once afforded,
But you never lose a friend!

Years may come and bring their sorrow,
Shape your courses far apart,
But the dawn of each tomorrow
Finds him nearer to your heart;
Time will bring a fuller measure
Of the happiness you've known,
Memories be yours to treasure
In the hours you spend alone.

He may cross the broadest ocean
And with strangers find abode,
Still the thought of his devotion
Lighter makes your daily load
Mother Earth may close above him,
As with all it soon must do,
But because 'twas yours to love him
Life is richer far for you!

MOTHER'S DAY

Why should Mother's Day be chosen
For just this time of year?
Why not in the dead of winter
Or in gray November drear?

Because the birds are singing
And there's green in yonder field,
And the apple trees in blossom
A pleasant perfume yield.

And what are fields in springtime
Spreading like a verdant sea,
But the promise of a harvest,
A harvest yet to be?

And what are apple blossoms
Lending fragrance to the air,
But the promise of the fruitage
That the good old trees will bear?

And thus the love of mother,
That abides through sun and gloom,
Is the promise of devotion
That will live beyond the tomb!

Then what could be more fitting
Than that Mother's Day should come
When the fields are green with promise
And the orchards are in bloom?

THE ANSWER

He was talking with his father
As most any boy will do,
Asking countless boyish questions
Ever old, yet ever new.

"I am growing, daddy, growing!
Will it always be this way,
And will God grow just as I do,
Just a little bit each day?"

There's an answer to his question,
"Yes indeed, He surely will,
He will be your greatest comfort
As you climb Life's thorny hill!

"But no matter how you struggle
You will never understand
How the earth and starry heavens
Fit so nicely in His hand!

"Though you grow in mind and spirit,
Strength and wisdom till the end,
He will always be far greater
Than your mind can comprehend!"

KNITTIN'

It seems to me a foolish thing
To spend the time embroidering,
A foolish thing to sit and tat,
To knit, crochet, and things like that;
They're wastin' time, now that's my thought,
A-makin' things that could be bought.

I never quite know which is which,
They just sit down and stitch and stitch,
Knit one, purl two or maybe three,
It's all a mystery to me;
Sometimes they knit and then crochet,
It's all the same thing anyway.

And yet, somehow there can't be found,
In searchin' all the country round,
Another picture quite so sweet,
That to the soul is such a treat
As mother hummin' soft and low,
A-knittin', rockin' to and fro!

TWO ROADS

Two roads lie just before you,
You are at the fork today,
One a downward path to darkness,
One an upward shining way.

Perhaps you've scarcely noticed
The distinction 'twixt the two;
At the start they seem so level
You may be deceived, it's true.

But the further you may travel
After your decision's made,
The greater the distinction,
And the steeper is the grade.

And yet, tho' long you've journeyed
On the low road or the high,
You can still change your direction
If you have a mind to try.

If for years your feet have faltered
A-down the darkening hill,
The change may seem much harder
But you'll make it, if you will.

Or perhaps you may have journeyed
On the upward path of light,
Yet the road is lined with byways,
You may yet go down to night.

Say to yourself each morning,
When preparing for the day,
"I am now, as I am always,
At the fork of life's great way."

THE MIXER

Now if I could be a mixer
Like some fellows I have found
And be always in the center
When a crowd is gathered 'round,
Then I wouldn't want a million
And I wouldn't ask for fame,
Wouldn't care for any title
To be written with my name.

For a man might have a title
And be sick at heart, it's true,
And a fellow with a million
Could be mighty lonesome too
If he had to stand forever
Just along the outer rim
Of the crowd, while genial fellows
Edged along ahead of him.

There's a door across the entrance
To the heart, that none may see,
And a hundred million dollars
Wouldn't turn its magic key,
But a cheery word of greeting
And a friendly smile will win,
For the door is always open
To the one who mixes in!

ENRAPTURED

There's a glory in the heavens
That no artist's brush reveals,
And no poet's pen expresses
All the wonderment he feels;
The majestic snow-clad mountain
And the prairie's rolling span
Put to shame the noblest effort
Of the puny mind of man!

In the bridge that spans the chasm
And the spire against the sky,
With the utmost skill and patience,
Man has sought to please the eye,
But when nature clothes the woodland
In the scarlet robes of fall,
Yonder maple on the hillside
Is more beautiful than all!

If I fail to see the beauty
In a lovely work of art,
Or the work of some Old Master
Somehow fails to touch my heart,
Should I miss the golden glory
Of the path some hero trod,
Please forgive me, I'm enraptured
By the Wondrous Works of God!

NOT GUILTY

When I stand before my Maker
In the better world on high,
To recount my many failures
And the sins done on the sly,
There'll be much to say against me
For I haven't been as true
To my duty as I should have;
Can't the same be said of you?

But I hope I'll not be guilty
Of perceiving only wrong
In my fellow human beings
As they slowly toiled along,
Nor of speaking of my neighbors
All the evil I could tell,
When a little word of kindness
Would have answered just as well!

IN THE SLEIGH

See the crowds of Christmas shoppers
Along the busy street;
Hear the din of passing autos,
The tread of rushing feet.

How changed from the Christmas shopping
We did in the long ago,
When we drove to town, behind the team,
In the sleigh, through drifted snow.

Grandfather drove, from the old spring seat,
While the rest of us sat behind,
In the old sleigh-box, our feet in the straw,
And our backs to the stormy wind.

Grandmother rode with the rest of us
Through the eight long miles to town;
The wind was keen, but the blankets snug,
And her courage would not down.

But the years that have come and departed
Have touched with a heavy hand,
And many of those who rode in the sleigh
Have gone to a brighter land.

No more will the old team canter
At grandfather's spoken word,
And grandmother's, "Merry Christmas" will
No more, in this life, be heard.

All thought of the crowd in the busy street
Will be passed and gone with the day,
But we'll never forget, while life shall last,
The crowd that rode in the sleigh.

RIDING ALONE

The sun sank low in the western hills,
The sky was cold and gray,
As slowly along the homeward trail,
Creaked an old, decrepit sleigh.

The team mismatched for color and gait,
The harness was worn and old,
And the sleigh itself seemed falling apart
As it creaked and groaned in the cold.

They didn't prance, as horses do
At the sound of sleighbells gay,
But plodded along, their heads bowed down,
Through the gathering twilight gray.

No bells, no sound of a merry voice,
There was nothing to cause a smile,
To brighten the journey, to lighten the load,
Or shorten the weary mile.

And the couple who rode thro' the deepening gloom,
Talked little—with voices low;
Their clothes were brought—so it seemed at least,
From out of the long ago.

Her shawl and gown were as out of date
As the coat and scarf he wore;
If you had seen them, you'd have said,
"They must be very poor."

And that is where you'd have been far wrong,
For on this long cold ride,
Not one alone, but the two of them,
Jogged onward, side by side.

And you may ride in a chartered car,
Or a limousine may own,
But you are poorer, by far, than they,
If you must ride—alone.

THE AFTER A WHILE

There's a beautiful river, the After A While,
With travelers drifting away;
It flows through the country of Putting Things Off,
Till it broadens out into the bay.

Far down at the mouth of this slow-winding stream
Is the city of Never, I hear,
And those who would drift on the eddying tide
Must tie at its tumbledown pier.

So if you wouldn't go to the city I've named,
Don't ask me the "why" or the "how";
Just portage today, to the stream o'er the hill,
That turbulent river, the "Now"!

WHERE THE RIVER'S STRONG

The river's a thing of beauty
Slow-winding a-down its way;
Bright-tinted with gold at sunset,
And calm at the close of day.
'Tis broad as the world, but shallow
As sands on a thorny steep,
But down in the rugged narrows
Ah! That's where the river's deep!

'Tis weak with the easy going,
And the current is laggard, slow;
'Tis roiled with the silt of ages
And tossed by the winds that blow;
But down where the channel narrows
It sings with a thund'rous song,
For down in the rugged narrows
Ah! That's where the river's strong!

PLANS

We lay our little foolish plans
As if we meant to stay
And down the corridor of years
We let our fancy stray.

But Lo! A greater mind than ours
Has laid the master plan,
A stronger, wiser hand, controls
The destiny of man!

Whatever fits this greater plan,
In many years or few,
Whatever task is there assigned,
That task is ours to do.

We lay our little foolish plans
As if we meant to stay;
Alas, we do not know the end
Of just one little day!

REALITY

I'm sorry for the boy today
Who never, never knows
The feel of shoeless feet on clay
And mud between his toes!

O yes, he has a cowboy suit,
A wide-rimmed hat and gun,
The gun, he knows full well won't shoot,
The clothes are just in fun.

A far, far cry from that old time
When came our biggest thrill,
And shoes removed, we'd gaily climb
The nearest sandy hill.

'Twas quite an honor then to be
The very first to go
In barefoot joy across the lea
So lately bare of snow.

Then as the summer quickly sped
Our feet, no longer white,
Would toughen till they'd almost shed
A thistle—but not quite!

So let him keep his make-believe,
His gun and cowboy ways,
But let my fancy fondly weave
Around those Barefoot Days!

MY BOYHOOD HOME

Two farms there are that together stand
In the self-same spot, on the self-same land;
Two farms? You'll tell me that I am wrong,
For you'll see but one as you pass along.

You'll see the farm as it is today
With its house remodeled in colors gay;
No eyes, save mine, in the world can see
The beloved old farm as it used to be.

For Dad and Mother are there no more,
And the trees that stood by the farmhouse door
Are gone, as gone are the friends who came
For an evening's pleasure or boyhood game.

The barn, the sheds, and the wall of stone
That has crumbled down as the years have flown,
Are gone or changed till you'd never know
'Twas the same old farm of the long ago.

The sun sinks low at the long day's close
In the same old hills that my fancy knows,
That sun, those hills, and the golden west
Have remained of all that I loved the best!

Just these, 'twould seem, are beyond the range
Of the endless battle with Time and Change;
They bridge the gap, in the twilight gloam,
From the farm you see—to my boyhood home!

THE NEW HOME

A house you have, and through the years
'Twill come to be a home,
The most beloved and finest place
Beneath the sky's blue dome,
For homes just aren't built of wood
Or brick and stone and tile,
But of materials that grow
With each succeeding mile.

And so, dear friends, we wish you well
Whatever may betide,
To us that house will be a place
Where those we love abide.
A place grown dearer with the love
Each fleeting year imparts,
Until it finds as deep a place
As you have, in our hearts!

THE OTHER DAY

You say 'twas long, long years ago
We whiled away the hours
Around the schoolhouse on the hill
Among the trees and flowers.

'Twas long ago we laughed and played
Nor knew a thought of care;
It must be true for there's a shade
Of silver in our hair.

The games we played, the lessons learned,
The good old friends we knew,
Are but a shadow of the past—
It can't, it can't be true!

Ah no! It can't be long, long years
For many things I know
That happened then seem nearer now
Than those a week ago.

The lines of care, the furrowed brow,
The thinning locks of gray
Can't make us feel 'twas long ago,
'Twas just the other day!

FAREWELL OLD TREES

Farewell, Old Trees! The dawn brings death
To keep his tryst with you;
Your giant forms must crash to earth
Before the logging crew!

Your silent aisles will know the din
Of woodsmen's axe and saw,
And feel the ruthless hand of man
Whose love of gold is law!

Farewell, Old Trees! The setting sun
Will search the barren plain,
Its last faint rays will seek to light
Your slender boughs—in vain!

The breath of May will fail to stir
Your forms so still and cold,
And autumn sun reflect no more
Your scarlet, brown, and gold.

O Time! Stretch forth thy healing hand
In kindness where they fell,
When other eyes than mine shall see,
Farewell, Old Trees! Farewell!

GIFTS

Again the bells of New Year chime
What hast for me this year, O Time?

Alas, thy gifts, O Time, to me
Must all too soon forgotten be.

That I am rich or famed or strong
Will not remembered be for long.

But if I bring rich gifts to Thee
In meekness and humility,

And strive to bring a brighter day
These gifts, O Time, will live for aye!

GOLD

O glittering yellow metal,
What power is in thy hand;
At thy word come years of plenty,
Or gaunt famine stalks the land.

Famine in the midst of plenty,
Nations poor with all they need,
Poor because their very living
Goes to satisfy thy greed.

Monarchs, statesmen, do thy bidding,
Men and nations are but pawn;
With thy swiftly passing fancy
Hope arises—and is gone.

When will man throw off the fetters
That have bound him through the years;
When emerge, at last triumphant,
From the ocean of his tears?

In his bitter fight for freedom,
That has now grown ages old,
Will he ever know—the shackles
That have bound him are of gold?!

JUST A PILGRIM

Home and friends, it seemed in childhood,
Were a blessing I could hold,
Would be with me, time unnoticed,
While the long years slowly rolled.

Youth and health would e'er be with me,
Age and change would never come,
Life was something never-ending,
And this world, I thought, was home.

But the years, alas, have taught me
Just how deeply I was wrong;
Now I know I'm just a pilgrim,
And I cannot tarry long.

Just a pilgrim on a journey
O'er a rough and troubled sea;
Father Time, the good ship's captain,
Ever beckons, "Come with me!"

JUST ONCE

Just once in the year do the geese fly south,
And once does the first snow fall,
Just once do the buds burst forth in spring,
And once does the corn grow tall!

Just once in the day does the purple East
Light up with the glow of dawn,
And once do the deepening shadows fall,
At dusk, when the sun is gone.

Then how can a person be tired of Life
Or bored in a world like ours?
Where once is the season of crimson leaves
And once is the time of flowers.

For so it is planned in the life of man,
His story is quickly told,
Just once he's a child at his mother's knee,
And once he is gray and old.

Then give me the wisdom, good Lord, to know
The miracles shown to me,
That I may watch any passing day—
Yet never again may see!

TIME'S MIRACLES

Not from boyhood in a moment,
Does a man emerge full-grown,
But through years of patient study
Are the ways of wisdom shown.

Page by page life's book is opened,
One by one its gates unfold;
Lock by lock the silver mingles
In the hair that once was gold.

Not in loose haphazard fashion
Are the tasks of manhood done,
But by years of toiling upward
Are the victor's laurels won.

Leaf by leaf the woods turn crimson,
One by one our old friends go;
Flake by flake our brows are whitened
With the drifts of time's deep snow.

Not in chaos or confusion
As a fortress battle stormed,
But in calm unerring order
Are time's miracles performed.

Bud by bud the spring awakens,
One by one new hopes are born;
Step by step the soul arises
To the dawn of Heaven's morn!

FRAILTY OF MAN

Man is vain and ever boastful
When the skies are clear and fair,
And his billowed sails swell gently
In the soft and balmy air;
It is then he thinks of power
And of riches he may gain,
Dreams his dream of fame and glory,
Boasts of skill and brawn and brain.

But when tempests, raging wildly,
Send the breakers rolling high,
And the heavens quake with thunder
As the lightning rends the sky,
Then his stature is as nothing,
Weak and frail his puny form,
He is small indeed and helpless
In the fury of the storm!

Ah! Then how much smaller is he
As he stands beneath the light
Of the blazing sun at noonday
Or the countless stars of night!
When a thousand worlds roll by him
In the canopy of skies,
And the wisdom of the ages
Hides beyond his sightless eyes!

MY TEMPLE

In the dead of night I slumbered
And a dream came to my sleep,
Like a sailor's dream of haven
When a storm is on the deep.

I beheld a Lofty Temple
Called "The Coming World of Peace,"
And upon it, this inscription,
"And the Din of War Shall Cease."

Stately pillars lent their beauty
And their strength to its support,
One was "Treaties." One "Agreements,"
And another's name was "Court."

On its spacious grounds were stationed
Mighty armies of the earth,
And the leaders of the nations
Proudly hailed its sterling worth.

From my dream of Peace and Plenty
I awakened with a start,
And a scene of desolation
Sent its terror to my heart!

For a sad defect I noticed
In my Temple, all too late,
And it lay in utter ruin
For its cornerstone was "Hate."

ONE VERSE

Suppose the Bible had been lost
And just one verse remained;
Which one of all the many there
Should be the one retained?

Some stern command, some awful threat
Of punishment for crime
Awaiting souls of guilty men
Beyond the realms of Time?

Or should it be a lovely verse,
That tells the matchless story
Of man's redemption—and his home
In everlasting glory?

Ah no! For in a few short lines
The meaning must be told;
The ageless lesson must be taught
In just one verse of gold!

So we must banish crime and guilt
And do away with fear,
And with the lesson we must bring
The Gates of Heaven near!

One verse, there is, that stands the test—
The Bible's richest gem—
"Whate'er ye would that men should do,
Do even so—to them."

TIME AND YOU

Do you see, good friend and neighbor,
One in yonder thorny lane,
Gray with years and bent with sorrow,
Leaning feebly on his cane?

He is weary with his burden,
Heavy heartache has he known,
With each step the path grows steeper
And the way more drear and lone!

Treat him kindly, ever mindful
Of the struggle he has seen,
Plant his feet on smoother going
Where the slope is broad and green.

Cause a smile to light his features,
Smooth the furrows from his brow,
For he's you, good friend and neighbor,
In a few short years from now!

PETITION TO TIME

I do not ask of thee, O Time,
That I should costly treasures own,
Nor that my wayward feet should climb
The golden stairway to a throne.

The heights of glory are attained
By stronger, wiser men than I,
The lofty peaks of triumph gained
By those who bravely live and die!

Content am I whatever task
Is mine, allotted from thy store,
If this one favor I shall ask
May granted be—I want no more!

Search then thy records and at last
Give me one day that I may know
And live again the silent past
And dream the dreams of long ago.

Bring back the oft-remembered friend,
The far-off places once so near
And by a touch of magic, blend
Tomorrow with some bygone year.

Recall the phantom that was youth,
Its joyous spirit, this I pray,
The simple childish faith in truth,
Bring back, O Time, Just One Brief Day!

MY BEQUEST

I shall not leave a vast estate
When life's swift race is run;
When at last I've made the crossing
At the setting of the sun.
No wealth, no power will e'er be mine,
I'll win no loud acclaim;
My name will ne'er be written
In the gilded hall of fame.

And yet, perchance, someone may pause
At some far-distant time,
To read a verse that I have left
Or sing a song of mine;
Let others leave their wealth and power,
I shall be satisfied
If I can leave a song that lives
When I have crossed the tide!